Do we have to k

stephen perse

foundation

Story written by Gill Munton
Illustrated by Tim Archbold

Speed Sounds

Consonants *Ask children to say the sounds.*

f	l	m	n	r	s	v	z	sh	th	ng
ff	ll	mm	nn	rr	ss	(ve)	zz			nk
ph	le		(kn)	wr	se		se			
					ce		s			

b	c	d	g	h	j	p	qu	t	w	x	y	ch
bb	k	dd	gg		g	(pp)		tt	(wh)			tch
	ck				ge							

Each box contains one sound but sometimes more than one grapheme.
*Focus graphemes for this story are **circled**.*

Vowels

Ask children to say the sounds in and out of order.

a	e ea	i	o	u	ay	(ee) y	igh i	ow o
at	hen	in	on	up	day	see	high	blow

oo	oo	ar	or oor ore	air	ir	ou	oy oi
zoo	look	car	for	fair	whirl	shout	boy

5

Story Green Words

Ask children to read the words first in Fred Talk and then say the word.

Dan Reed   heels   eel   dumps   combats   guess*   both*   wash*

Ask children to say the syllables and then read the whole word.

in|sect   sett|ee   sec|onds   greed|y   carr|ot   slopp|y

pre|tend*   al|most*   sis|ter*   ev|er|y*

Ask children to read the root first and then the whole word with the suffix.

wheel → wheels

* Challenge Words

6

Vocabulary Check

Discuss the meaning (as used in the story) after the children have read each word.

	definition:	**sentence:**
stick insect	an insect that you can keep as a pet	I wanted a stick insect.
settee	sofa	Mum sits on the settee.
eel	an underwater snake-like animal	It's not a baby at all – it's an eel!
dumps	drops down, puts	Then Mum dumps the baby on my knee.
combats	trousers	It wees on my best combats!
creep	goody goody	My sister Sheena is just a creep.

Red Words

Ask children to practise reading the words across the rows, down the columns and in and out of order clearly and quickly.

want	all	one	to
do	you	I'm	I've
baby	was	were	of
one	they	your	call
what	school	said	are

Do we have to keep it?

I'm Dan Reed.
I'm almost ten, and I live at
fifteen, Fleetwood Street.
And I've got ... a baby!

Well, Mum and Dad have.
And I'm not feeling very happy.
I did tell Mum that I wanted a stick insect,
but no, she went and got a baby.
And no, it cannot go back to the shop!

This baby! It looks very funny.
You want to see it!

Mum sits on the settee,
and sticks the baby on her knee.
It digs its heels into her legs,
and then it kicks with both feet
and twists its body.
It's not a baby at all – it's an eel!

Then the baby needs feeding.
It seems to need feeding every three seconds,
it's so greedy.

Bits of mashed up beef and carrot,
yuk, and milk, milk, milk.

Oh, yes, and it's got this silly bib
with a green sheep on it!

Then Mum dumps the baby on my knee,
so she can wash up the lunch dishes.
The next thing is, it's sick on the sheep bib,
or it wees on my best combats!
I ask Mum, do we have to keep it?

My sister Sheena (she's sixteen)

is just a creep. She gives the baby a
big sloppy kiss, then mops it up with
a flannel, and puts it in its buggy.

We set off along Fleetwood Street.
Sheena wheels the buggy, and I pretend
I'm not with them.

If we meet Val from next door,
she greets us with,
"Oh! He's just sooooo sweet!"
No one tells me I'm sweet.
(Not that I want them to.)

When we get back, it's six o'clock and
the baby has to go to bed. Mum sticks it
in its cot – and sings to it!
It's got a pink teddy
that bleeps if you press its tummy.

When it's asleep, at last,
we have a bit of a rest from it.
Then it's "Eeeeeeeee! Wheeeeeeee!"
and guess what – it's been sick on the sheets.

Yippee! I'm going out for a meal with Dad today.
Just him and me. No baby ...

But I may get the baby a new toy, or a silly hat.
I've got a funny feeling that I'll miss him, just a teeny-weeny bit.

Questions to talk about

Ask children to TTYP each question using 'Fastest finger' (FF) or 'Have a think' (HaT).

p.9 (FF) What did Dan want instead of a baby?

p.10 (FF) What animal does Dan think the baby is like?

p.11 (FF) How often does Dan say the baby needs feeding?

p.12 (FF) What happens to Dan's best combats?

p.13 (FF) What does Val from next door say to the baby?

p.14 (FF) Why does the baby start crying?

p.15 (HaT) Why might Dan buy something for the baby?

Questions to read and answer

(Children complete without your help.)

1. What number is Dan's house in Fleetwood Street?
   Dan Reed lives at number **ten / six / fifteen** Fleetwood Street.

2. What sort of pet did Dan want?
   Dan wanted **a puppy / a kitten / a stick insect**.

3. What food did the baby like?
   The baby liked **ham and eggs / mashed up beef and carrots / bread and jam**.

4. What animal is on the baby's bib?
   The baby has a bib with **a green sheep / a pink pig / a red hen** on it.

5. Who does Dan go out for a meal with?
   Dan goes out with **the baby / his dad / his sister**.

Speedy Green Words

Ask children to practise reading the words across the rows, down the columns and in and out of order clearly and quickly.

funny	feeding	knee	body
creep	sheets	live	feeling
very	three	milk	best
next	door	sweet	pink
asleep	just	happy	lunch